The Great Conspiracy

THE GREAT CONSPIRACY.
AND
ENGLAND'S NEUTRALITY.

MR. JAY'S ADDRESS

At Mount Kifco, New York,

The Fourth of July, 1861.

THE GREAT CONSPIRACY.

AN ADDRESS

Delivered at Mt. Kisco, West Chester County, New York,
on the 4th of July, 1861,

The 86th Anniversary of American Independence.

BY

JOHN JAY, esq.

NEW–YORK:

ROE LOCKWOOD & SON, 411 BROADWAY.

LONDON :—TRÜBNER & CO.

1861.

THE GREAT CONSPIRACY.

Mr. Jay's Address.

My Fellow-Countrymen :—

We have assembled to celebrate the eighty-sixth birth-day of American independence, and we come together under circumstances that seem to make us contemporaries and co-actors as it were, with our fathers of the revolution. The crisis which they met, and which their heroism decided after a seven years' war with Great Britain, again meets us face to face. The early scenes of their struggle for constitutional liberty, have found in our recent experience an historic parallel of even chronological exactness.

The blood of Massachussetts, shed at Lexington on the 19th of April 1775, was not shed more gloriously than that of the sons of the same old commonwealth, who, marching by our national highway, to the defence of our common capital, were slain at Baltimore on the 19th of April, 1861.

The midnight ride of Paul Revere, famed in history and song, rousing the sleepers as he passed to hasten to defend their country, created no deeper emotion among the colonists of that day, than did our electric wires flashing far and wide the news of the assault on Sumpter and the massacre at Baltimore, and thrilling with a simultaneous burst of sympathy the loyal heart of the American people.

On the 4th of July 1776, the congress that met in the state house at Philadelphia approved the solemn instrument that declared the independence of the American colonies, and announced to the world the birth of a nation. Eighty-five years have rolled by : the actors in that eventful scene have long since gone to

their graves : their names belong to history : their sons have
grown to manhood and age and have followed them to the unseen
world : and we of the third and fourth generation occupy the
stage they trod, and represent the nationality which then was
born. Eighty-five years of almost uninterrupted prosperity and
unexampled growth! eighty-five years of culture and experience
in a century of progress such as the world has never seen before !
eighty-five years of thoughtful reflection on the character of the
men who laid the foundation of our national glory and of the
broad principles of right on which they based the edifice of American freedom!

Those years have passed ; their results are written on the map
of America, on the page of history, and to-day, the 4th of July
1861, the American congress convenes again at the call of the
president at the capital bearing the name of Washington, to
meet the question, whether the republic is to be maintained in
its integrity with the constitution proclaimed by Washington
based on the will of the majority, or whether it is to be sundered
and shattered by a defeated faction that sets at defiance the will
of the people and would trample the constitution in the dust.

If ever the spirits of the departed are permitted to revisit the
scenes they loved, and hover like angels around the steps of their
successors, we may suppose that Hancock, and the Adamses,
Sherman and Wolcott, Carroll and Livingston, Jefferson and
Franklin, Robert and Lewis Morris, Wilson and Rush, and all
their noble compeers, look down from heaven in this hour upon
the Congress at Washington ; and God grant that the sturdy
spirit which inspired the first Congress may equally inspire the
last !

" Whatever may be our fate," said John Adams, with prophetic
vision, after the adoption of the declaration,—" be assured that
this declaration will stand. It may cost treasure and it may cost
blood, but it will richly compensate for both. Through the thick
gloom of the present I see the brightness of the future as the
sun in heaven. We shall make this a glorious, an immortal day.
When we are in our graves our children will honuor it. They will
celebrate it with thanksgiving, with festivities, with bon-fires
with illuminations. On its annual return they will shed tears, no·

of subjection and slavery, not of agony and distress, but of exultation, of gratitude and of joy. Sir, before God, I believe the hour is come : all that I have, all that I am, all that I hope for in this life, I am now ready here to stake upon it, and I leave off as I began, that live or die, sink or swim, survive or perish, I am for the declaration. It is my living sentiment, and by the blessing of God it shall be my dying sentiment,—Independence now, and independence forever!"

The integrity and independence of our country are again in peril, and to-day the issue is with us. We come together now, not as in past years, to rejoice over a national domain boundless in extent, peopled by countrymen differing, it may be in their views and institutions but united in loyalty and affection, at peace in their own borders, and with the great arm of the union protecting its citizens alike on sea or land, at home or in foreign climes. But we meet in sadness to overlook a divided nation, and to listen to tne tramp of martial forces larger than ever before trod the soil of America : the one army bearing proudly aloft the stars and stripes, and keeping step to the music of the union ; the other grasping the banner of rebellion and the black flag of piracy, proclaiming death to the constitution and the union, and ruin to the commerce of the republic.

Several states, about one-fourth of our whole number, profess to have resumed their sovereignty and *seceded*, as they term it from the federal union : and certain persons professing to act in their name, have extemporized what they call the Southern Confederacy, elected a president, Jefferson Davis, and a vice-president, Alexander H. Stephens, organized an army. issued letters of marque. and declared war on the people and the government of the United States : and they have publicly announced, through Walker, the secretary of Davis, their intention of speedily seizing our capital at Washington, with its national archives and muniments of title.

To meet the rebel force arrayed against the capital, president Lincoln has called upon the loyal states, and at the word, fresh from the plow, the loom and the workshop, fresh from college seats and the professor's chair, from the bar, the pulpit, and the counting house, fresh from every department of American industry, the army of the union is in the field, and the world awaits the impending crisis. Europe looks on with undisguised and wondering interest, and while France and Germany seem instinctively to appreciate our situation, the British cabinet and the British press have strangely blundered, and have muttered something we do not understand, about "rights of belligerents," "a wicked war," and the "bursting of the bubble of democracy."

Such, in brief, is our position at home and abroad, and this day is destined to be memorable—perhaps as memorable in history as that which we have met to celebrate. The action of the congress now assembled will decide whether the national independence established against the united strength of the British empire in '76 is to fall ignominiously before the attacks of a rebel minority of our own countrymen in '61.

It is to decide the question whether in the next century our descendants shall refer to the fourth of July as the forgotten birth-day of an extinct republic, or whether, when we shall sleep with our fathers and our children shall slumber by our side, their grandsons shall meet as we do this day to bless our memories as we bless those of our revolutionary sires : to spread to the breeze from the Atlantic to the Pacific, on every hill side and in every valley, the flag of our union, the stars and stripes that we so proudly love, and join their voices in swelling the cry of Adams—"Independence now, and independence forever !"

While the great issue, the success or failure of the American experiment, the continuance of our union or its disintegration rests immediately with the president and with congress, it rests in an almost equal degree upon each one of us. The American people are at once citizens and sovereigns—the fountain and source of the supreme authority of the land, and to us the people, will our servants in congress naturally and properly look for guidance in this extremity. Already have you seen how fairly an honest executive represents the sentiments of the majority of his countrymen, availing himself of their counsels, gathering strength from their energy and determination, and so directing the government that its action keeps time to the beating of the national pulse. Already in response to the nation's call has the national government arisen in gigantic strength from the depths of imbecility to which it had fallen, to a position of grandeur, dignity and power, which has silenced the half uttered sarcasms of European declaimers about the internal weakness of popular institutions.

Most of you—perhaps all of you have made up your minds deliberately, intelligently and dispassionately in regard to your duty ; and it is a general and proper sentiment among us that this is a time for energetic action, not for discussion. But still as I am here, honoured by your appointment to say something befitting the occasion, I think you will permit me, if indeed you do not regard it as my especial province, to speak frankly of our present duty ; to say something of the great theme which engrosses the nation ; of which we think when we rise in the morning and when we retire at night, as we go to our work and return to our meals, when we open the morning paper for news and close it for reflection, when we kneel at the family altar and by our own bed sides,—the one great overwhelming subject, the issue of this rebellion, the destiny of our country.

I can speak to you about it more familiarly, perhaps, than I should speak to strangers, for you are familiar with the whole matter, you know by heart the history of the revolutionary war in which the county of Westchester bore from the beginning so prominent a part, and from boyhood our thoughts and associations have been intimately connected with the facts of our colonial dependence and the incidents that marked the struggle by which that dependence was at length terminated. Let me refer for an instant to some of the local memories which linger all around us. On the angle of Connecticut which juts into the State of New York, close by this town of Newcastle, stands the boundary rock, still bearing the initials "G. R.," brief memento of King George III., whose sovereignty over our fathers, loyal subjects though they were, and backed as was the crown by the armies of Great Britain, faded before the steadfastness of their resistance to unconstitutional usurpation.

New York in '76 being selected by the British as the centre of their operations, commanding, as they did, the Hudson river,

and acting in connection with a force from Canada, their march
into Westchester was designed to control the two principal
routes to New England, by the way of Rye and Bedford, and so
cut off the American army from its eastern supplies. Washing
ton, penetrating their designs, skilfully conducted his forces
northwardly from King's bridge, moving in a line parallel with
the British, keeping a little in advance, facing them constantly
with the Bronx in his front, the banks of the stream being for-
tified in convenient places.

I need not remind you of the battle of White Plains on the
28th October, 1776, where Alexander Hamilton distinguished
himself as a captain of artillery, nor of the heights of Newcastle, to which Washington repaired after the battle. At Bedford, where we hold our farms under Indian titles bearing the
mark of Katonah sagamore, that were confirmed by patent of
Queen Anne, some houses were burned in '79 by lieut. colonel
Tarlton, heading a detachment of the Queen's rangers, as related
in his despatch to Sir Guy Carleton. At Poundridge and Hitch-
ing's corner occurred bloody skirmishes. Then, there are near
by us Mile-square, where the Americans kept a strong guard ;
Pine's bridge, which served as the principal communication between the hostile lines, and where Enoch Crosby, the Westchester spy—known to all readers of our great novelist as Har-
vey Birch, commenced his career of secret service ; King's
bridge, the barrier of the British lines on the Harlem river,
commanded in New York by Lord Cathcart, where the cowboys
made their rendezvous when they had plundered the surround-
ing hills, and where a battle was fought between the Continen-
tals and the Hessians. Indeed the whole of the "neutral
ground," as pourtrayed by Fennimore Cooper, extending to the
Croton, the banks of the Hudson, Northcastle and Salem. connected with the sad drama of André and the, till recently un-
surpassed treason of Arnold, all abound with revolutionary incidents ; not forgetting Valentine's hill at Mile-square. where
Washington was encamped in '76, Sir William Erskine in '78
and where in '82, as Mr. Bolton tells us, a grand foray was made
with some 6,000 men by Sir Guy Carleton in person. attended

among other officers of note by the young duke of Clarence, afterwards William the fourth.

Dwelling as you do amid scenes so suggestive, there should be no traitors in Westchester unless indeed, they are the descendants of the cow-boys and skinners, those pests of the Revolution, who were at once selfish, treacherous, cowardly, and cruel ; and if any traitors should again be found in our borders—men ready for their own selfish interests to betray either the national principles, or the national integrity that our fathers bought for us at so great a price, do not forget to remind them that the "Cow-boy oak" yet stands near Yonkers, on which their traitorous ancestors were suspended with "a short shrift and a sure cord ;" and that equally patriotic oaks in every part of Westchester send forth their broad arms ready to perform for our country, should its safety at any time unhappily demand it, the same excellent service.

You are familiar also with the history of our Constitution, and with those marked lines of distinction between the authority of the States and that of the Federal government, which to some of the statesmen and authors of England seem so difficult of comprehension, and in regard to which perhaps naturally enough, they occasionally fall into blunders, which unfortunately are not always as harmless as the droll liberties they are accustomed to take with our history, our geography, and our nomenclature.

If ever the constitutional history of America shall receive in the education of English gentlemen a tithe of the attention bestowed on the constitutions of Greece and Rome, or a share of that devoted to the fabulous heroes, the gods and goddesses of classic mythology, the British senate may occasionally find a familiarity with our institutions of no slight value, especially if it shall save them from rashly interrupting the cordial friendship of a kindred people.

The universality of such knowledge here, makes us perhaps more ready to remark the want of it in foreign critics. Dr. Franklin said during the last century, and the progress of education and improvements in our newspapers have made the remark more true of the present than of the past;—" we are more thoroughly an enlightened people, with regard to our political interests than perhaps any other under heaven."

You remember that in 1774 the members of the first congress at Philadelphia, on behalf of the colonies which they represented, entered into certain articles of association "under the sacred ties of virtue, honour and love of country." That in 1778 the states united in a confederacy, or what they called "a firm league of friendship with each other," under the title of the United States, and that under this league made by the states, they continued until 1789, when, "in order to form a more perfect union"— not the states—but "We the people of the United States" ordained and established the present federal constitution. You remember that from the date of the peace in '83, when we were a mere league of petty sovereignties, we sank rapidly, in the words of Mr. Motley, whose conclusive essay in the London *Times* has enlightened Europe, "into a condition of utter impotence, imbecility and anarchy," which continued until we were rescued from it by "The constitution of the United States," which made us, in every sense, one nation—with one supreme government, although for convenience, we retained the plural title under which we had achieved our independence of "The United States."

Any argument, therefore, addressed to you upon the constitutional right alleged by the rebels, of a state to secede from the union would be quite superfluous. Men have been allowed to talk of state sovereignty as it liked them, because ours is a free country and in ordinary times the utmost liberty of speech is permissible, but the doctrine has not even a respectable foothold. Washington, as if foreseeing the evil it has assisted to bring forth, denounced it as "that monster, state sovereignty." Webster and Jackson successively demolished it, and the argument now insolently advanced by leaders of the rebel states, that in seceding from the Union and seizing its property, they are only exercising their reserved rights under the Constitution, is one which to every intelligent and loyal American carries with it its own refutation.

The man who attaches to it the weight of a feather, is either

singularly ignorant of American history, or his reasoning powers
are hopelessly perverted.

The rebels, despite their pretended plea of constitutional right,
virtually admit its groundlessness, and fall back on the right of
revolution. That is a right which no American can deny, when
the causes of justification are sufficient. The simple cry of rebel
and revolutionist has no terror for us who remember that
Washington and our ancestors occupied the position of both the
one and the other.

All then depends upon the reality and sufficiency of the as-
signed causes of this attempt at revolution. Are they such as
to justify the effort to break in pieces the American union? to
destroy this last experiment of popular government?

The arguments offered by the insurrectionists and their friends,
to shew that the federal government and the loyal states should
quietly allow them to depart and form a separate confederacy
are these :

That the rebellion or revolution is the act of the people of
those states exercising their sovereign will.

That they have been compelled to this step in self defence by
the election of Mr. Lincoln, and the refusal of certain Northern
states to fulfil the constitutional obligation of returning fugitive
slaves.

That the present position of the rebels, and the fact of their
having ousted the federal government from its forts, and other
property, exhibit their strength, make the revolution an accomplished fact, and render the attempt to subjugate the Southern
people utterly hopeless.

That even if they were subjugated, harmonious feeling could
never be restored, and that for these reasons, and especially the
last, a war to maintain the integrity of the union would be alike
wicked and foolish.

These, I believe, are their strong points fairly stated, and I will
briefly state some of the grounds on which we believe them to
be, one and all, erroneous and delusive.

In the first place, the fact is clear that the rebellion at the
South was not in its inception like the rebellion of the American
colonies,—a calm, deliberate, determined, movement of the peo-

ple ; but that it was a conspiracy originating with a few ambitious politicians, and was by them suddenly precipitated upon the people, whose right to pass upon their acts of secession has been purposely, systematically and practically denied. "There is," said Webster,—and his words were never before so fearfully illustrated,—"no usurpation so dangerous as that which comes in the borrowed name of the people ; which calling itself their servant, exercises their power without legal right or constitutional sanction."

You all remember the stern rebukes uttered by the Southern press, of the rash precipitancy of South Carolina, and the efforts made by their prominent statesmen, among whom Mr. Stephens was one, to stay the efforts of the rebel leaders to plunge the South into rebellion. Even after several states had by their conventions,—and the convention of Louisiana was elected by a a minority of the people—been declared out of the union ; and after delegates from those conventions had met in congress at Montgomery, and extemporized their new confederacy, the bolder part of the Southern press did not hesitate to denounce the usurpation.

The "Augusta Chronicle and Sentinel"—a leading paper of Georgia—openly declared that the result had been produced by "wheedling, coaxing and bullying, and all the arts of deception." It said :

"We know as well as any one living that the whole movement for secession and the formation of a new government, so far at least as Georgia is concerned, proceeded only on a *quasi* consent of the people, and was pushed through under circumstances of great excitement and frenzy by a fictitious majority." And then passing to the Montgomery congress, it added :

"The Georgia convention and the confederate congress have gone forward in their work, as none can deny, without explicit and direct authority from the people." * * * "It is time that this assumption of power should cease, and that the people should be heard. Sooner or later they must be heard. * * * Before the convention assumes to ratify the permanent constitution let them submit it to a vote of the people—or else, let us have an election for a new convention. For union—for harmony —for strength—we ask this simple act of justice."

Simple justice was not the aim of Jefferson Davis and his co-conspirators. To this day the people of the South have been allowed no opportunity of passing upon the profoundest question that can affect a nation—the preservation or overthrow of its institutions; and the rebel government is an usurpation of the grossest kind, not only against the people of the United States in their sovereign capacity, but against the people of the States in whose name it assumes to act, and by whose will it pretends to have been established.

The declaration, so solemnly made by the seceding conventions, appealing to the world for the justice of their cause, that Mr. Lincoln's election, the non-execution of the fugitive slave law, and the personal liberty laws of northern States, compelled them to separate from a government that threatened their dearest rights, is equally disproven out of their own mouths. Listen to the following utterances from the very leaders of the rebellion :

MR. RHETT said :—" The secession of South Carolina is not the event of a day. It is not anything produced by Mr. Lincoln or by the non-execution of the fugitive slave law. It is a matter which has been gathering head for years."

MR. PARKER.—" It is no spasmodic effort that has come suddenly upon us, but it has been gradually culminating for a long series of years."

MR. KEITT.—I have been engaged in this movement ever since I entered political life."

MR. INGLIS.—Most of us have had this matter under consideration for the the last twenty years."

That these declarations had a broad basis of truth, and that a plot to destroy the union has been hatching for a long period and has been deferred only until a convenient opportunity, is no longer a matter of speculation. The election of Mr. Lincoln was not the cause but only the occasion. Mr. Everett, in a recent lettter said, that he was "well aware, partly from facts within his personal knowledge, that leading Southern politicians had for thirty years been resolved to break up the union as soon as they ceased to control the United States government, and that the slavery question was but a pretext for keeping up agitation and rallying the South."

The Richmond Enquirer in 1856, declared, " If Fremont is elected the union will not last an hour after Mr. Pierce's term expires," and a careful examination will shew that from the attempt at nullification by South Carolina in 1832, which was defeated by the stern determination of General Jackson that the " union must and shall be preserved," a sentiment that was enthusiastically responded to by the country at large the design has been secrotly cherished, by a knot of conspirators at the South, of destroying the union whenever the men entertaining this design should no longer be able to control its government. So long as they could enjoy its honors and emoluments, and use its prestige, its treasury, its army and its navy for their own purposes, they were content that it should stand ; but the moment these were wrested from their grasp by the will of the people, that moment the union was to be destroyed.

So long ago as the year 1799 Judge Marshall in a letter to Washington, dated at Richmond, remarked :

" To me it seems that there are men who will hold power by any means rather than not hold it, and who would prefer a dissolution of the union to the continuance of an administration not of their own party." And Mr. Stephens declared in regard to the present conspiracy that the ambition of disappointed officeseekers constituted " a great part of the trouble.

General Jackson, after the South Carolina rebellion of 1832 was suppressed, foretold its attempted revival at no distant period, remarking that "the first time the pretence was the tariff, and that next it would be the negro question."

In 1836, twenty-five years ago, a political novel called the " Partizan Leader," was published by Professor Beverly Tucker, of William and Mary College, in Virginia. It excited no sensation then, but it possesses a singular interest now. It proceeds upon the theory that the events it describes as then happening would happen twenty years after, that is, in 1856, when Fremont would have probably been elected but for the frauds in Pennsylvania ; and it gives, with singular accuracy, the programme of the conspiracy which is now in progress. The author describes the southern states as seceding "by a movement nearly simultaneous," and immediately forming a southern confederacy. Let me quote a single paragraph :

"The suddenness of these measures was less remarkable than the prudence with which they had been conducted. The two together left little doubt that there had been a preconcert among the leading men of the several states, arranging previously what should be done. * * Nor was it confined to the seceding states alone. In Virginia also there were men who entered into the same views. * * Not only had they sketched provisionally the plan of a southern confederacy, but they had taken measures to regulate their relations with foreign powers."

What a flood of light is thrown upon the conspiracy by these few words from one of the earliest of the conspirators, who seems to have anticipated in part the rôle to be played by his own state of Virginia.

There being indications of her ultimate accession to the confederacy, the author says :

"The leading men" referred to "had determined to wait for her no longer, but to proceed to the execution of their plans, leaving her to follow."

Could the acute novelist have anticipated the proceedings of the pseudo-peace convention and the conduct of Virginia traitors, headed by an ex-President Tyler and an ex-Governor Wise, he might have eulogised the leaders of the ancient dominion for their treacherous skill in deluding the country with schemes of compromise while the preparations of the rebels were advancing to completion.

Mr. Everett, who was a warm **advocate** for the peace convention, has told us that "those conciliatory demonstrations had no effect in staying the progress of secession, because the leaders of that revolution were determined not to be satisfied."

In reference to the measures referred to by Professor Tucker, looking towards the relations of the now confederacy with foreign powers, it may be worth while to allude to a recent statement, that in the days of Mr. Calhoun a plan for the dissolution of the union and the formation of a great slaveholding power, was presented by his friends to Lord Aberdeen, and that some words attributed to that statesman, are supposed to have given rise to the hopes of British sympathy, in which southern politicians have so frequently indulged. It is said on high authority that at different times, and especially in 1851, these projects have been broached to members of the British ministry, and that on that occasion they were disclosed by Lord Palmerston to our minister, Mr. Abbott Lawrence, and that the southern commissioners disheartened by the coolness with which their overtures were received, and also by the fate of the Lopez expedition, returned discomfited to the United States.

In 1857 Mr. Mason, of Virginia, announced as a fact, on the floor of the senate, that the British government had changed its opinion on the slavery question, but an early occasion was taken by that government to contradict the assertion of Mr. Mason, the Duke of Argyll declaring that he was instructed by her Majesty's ministers to do so.*

Blind as we have all been to the catastrophe that awaited us, unconscious as were the people, both at the north and at the south, of this preconcert among a few leaders in the different states, we can now trace step by step the progress of the conspiracy and read the history of the last thirty years without an interpreter ; we can understand the motive of the Texan rebellion, the war with Mexico, the persistent efforts to secure Cuba, the fillibustering expeditions to Central America and the determination to re-open the African slave trade. We can appreciate, too, the caution with which the plan of the rebellion was concealed, and especially the adroitness with which the people were allowed no time for reflection, no opportunity for action, their consent assumed on the plea of necessary haste, and the acts of secession pushed through the conventions, as charged by the Georgian editor, with no regard to popular rights and under circumstances of excitement and frenzy by fictitious majorities.

The doctrine of secession, earnestly as it had been advocated, failed to convince the capitalists, the planters, and the common-sense statesmen of the South—even in South Carolina.

A few years since Mr. Boyce of that State, late a member of

* See a letter dated London, December 10, 1858, published and endorsed by the *Commercial Advertiser*, January 30, 1861.

the house of representatives, in an address to the people, after shewing that by secession they would lose the vitality of a state, that they would exist only by tolerance, a painful and humiliating spectacle, that it would involve a sacrifice of the present without in anywise gaining in the future, emphatically declared, "such is the intensity of my conviction on the subject, that if secession should take place, of which I have no idea, for I cannot believe in such stupendous madness, I shall consider the institution of slavery as doomed, and that the great God in our blindness has made us the instrument of its destruction."

Even so late as the autumn of 1860 and after the presidential election that announced the defeat of the slave power which had so long ruled the country, the leading men of the South who had not been in the plot battled manfully against it. On the 14th of November last, Mr. Stephens of Georgia, now the vice-president of the rebel confederacy, delivered a long and able speech in the Georgia house of representatives in which, in answer to the question whether the Southern states should secede in consequence of Mr. Lincoln's election, he said :

"My countrymen, I tell you frankly, candidly, and earnestly, that I do not think that they ought."

Reminding them of the sacred obligation resting on them to be true to their national engagements, he exclaimed :

"If the republic is to go down, let us be found to the last moment standing on the deck, with the Constitution of the United States waving over our heads." And this sentiment was greeted with applause,

He expressed his belief that Mr. Lincoln would do nothing to jeopard their safety or security, and shewed them the wisdom of our system with its checks and guards. He reminded them that the president was powerless unless backed by congress—that the house of representatives was largely against him, and that there would be a majority of four against him in the senate, and referring to a remark that no Georgian, who was true to his state, could consistently hold office under Mr. Lincoln, reminded them that such office could be honorably held, for it would be conferred by the approval of a democratic senate—and this exposition was received with "prolonged applause."

Mr. Stephens frankly avowed that he would never submit to any republican aggression on their constitutional rights to preserve the union, but insisted that all their rights could be secured in the union, and emphatically declared, " That this government of our fathers with all its defects, comes nearer the objects of all good governments than any other on the face of the earth, is my settled conviction." * * " Have we not at the South, as well as at the North, grown great, prosperous, and happy under its operation ? Has any part of the world ever shewn such rapid progress in the development of wealth, and all the material resources of national power and greatness as the Southern States have under the general government, notwithstand-all its defects ?"

Mr. Stephens then, with philosophic skill, shewed that the institutions of a people constitute the matrix from which spring all their characteristics of development and greatness. " Look," he said, " at Greece. There is the same fertile soil, the same blue sky, the same inlets and harbours, the same Egean, the same Olympus ; there is the same land where Homer sung, where Pericles spoke ; it is the same old Greece—but it is living Greece no more." He pictured its ruin of art and civilization, and traced that ruin to the downfall of their institutions. He drew the same lesson from Italy and Rome, once mistress of the world, and solemnly warned them that where liberty is once destroyed it may never return again.

Coming back to the state of Georgia he referred to the anxiety of many there in 1850 to secede from the Union — and shewed that since 1860 the material wealth of Georgia, as a member of the Union, had nearly if not quite doubled.

He spoke of the prosperity in agriculture, commerce, art, science, and every department of education, physical and mental, and warned them against listening to the like temptation as that offered to our progenitors in the Garden of Eden—when they were led to believe that they would become as gods, and yielding in an evil hour saw only their own nakedness.

" I look," he said, " upon this country, with its institutions, as the Eden of the world, the paradise of the universe. It may be that out of it we may become greater and more prosperous ; but

I am candid and sincere in telling you, that I fear if we rashly evince passion and without sufficient cause shall take that step, that instead of becoming greater or more peaceful, prosperous and happy — instead of becoming gods, we will become demons, and at no distant day commence cutting one another's throats."

Then, my countrymen, we have the testimony of the vice-president of the rebel confederacy, and the fact that Mr. Stephens, like our progenitors of whom he spoke, yielded to temptation and became a chief abettor of the scheme of ruin which he so strongly deprecated, detracts nothing from the value of this remarkable speech. His treachery proves only his own weakness, it impeaches neither the truth of his facts—the aptness of his illustrations nor the conclusions to which he was led by his historic experience and irresistible logic.

Already in South Carolina, first and chiefest of the seceding states, have men professing to be respectable, men whose names connect them in past generations, with Englishmen of gentle blood and Huguenots of heroic fame, men who for years have borne in foreign climes the proud title of American citizens, and who know the simple dignity of the American republic among the nations of the earth, — already are these men, since they discarded the protection of the federal government, so lost to self respect that they are not only ready to submit to a foreign yoke but, according to their eulogist, Mr. Russell, in a paragraph I will presently quote, they actually whimper like children for the privilege of becoming the vassals of an European princelet.

We have glanced at the secret history of the conspiracy. Now, let me ask, on what ground does this usurping confederacy ask to be recognized as independent and admitted to the family of nations?

In the convention of South Carolina, in reply to an objection that the declaration reported by the committee dwelt too much on the fugitive slave law and personal liberty bills, as giving it the appearance of special pleading, Mr. Memminger said : " Allow me to say to the honorable gentleman, that when you take position that you have a right to break your faith, to destroy an agreement that you have made, to tear off your seal from the document to which it is affixed, you are bound to justify yourself fully to all the nations of the world, for there is nothing that that casts such a stain upon the escutcheon of a nation as a breach of faith."

In this Mr. Memminger was clearly right, and the alleged breach of faith by the North, touching the execution of the fugitive slave law was resorted to as affording a plausible pretext for seceding from the union. But the debates shew that this pretext was a sham, and Mr. Rhett frankly declared that he regarded the fugitive slave law as unconstitutional, and that Mr. Webster and Mr. Keitt had expressed the same opinion.

You have seen, too, from Mr. Stephens, that all the constitutional rights of the South were protected within the union—and that the South was indebted to the union for her safety, prosperity and happiness.

What then is the real ground on which the breach of faith committed by the seceding states is to be justified, if it can be justified at all; on what ground is it recommended to the prejudices of the South and to the impartial judgment of the world?

After secession was an accomplished fact, so far as their conventions could manage it by usurped authority and fictitious majorities, and Mr. Stephens had become not only a member but a prominent leader of the conspiracy, he said at Atlanta:

"The foundations of our new government are laid, its cornerstone rests upon the great truth that the negro is not equal to the white man; that slavery, subordination to the superior race is his natural and moral condition. This our new government is the first in the history of the world based upon this great physical, philosophical and moral truth."

Mr. Stephens enlarged upon this distinguishing characteristic of the government, to establish which the union was to be dissolved, sneered at the principle that all men are equal, enunciated by our fathers in the declaration of independence "as the pestilent heresy of fancy politicians"—declared that "African inequality and the equality of white men were the chief cornerstone of the southern republic!" and claimed that with a government so founded "the world would recognize in theirs the the model nation of history."

Here we have their only apology for this rebellion, stripped of all shams and disguises, and thus at length in the latter half of the nineteenth century, stand face to face in deadly conflict the antagonist systems of the new world.

" All men," said the founders of the American republic, " are created free and equal and endowed with certain inalienable rights among which are life, liberty, and the pursuit of happiness." " Let it ever be remembered," said the continental congress, " that the rights for which we have contended were the rights of human nature," and on that foundation arose the fair fabric of our liberties.

The dark shadow arises of another confederacy which Davis and Keitt and Floyd and Toombs are striving to establish on the ruins of the republic erected by Washington and Franklin and Hamilton and Jefferson, and the one great plea with which this new power seeks to recommend itself to the Christian world, is the assumption that the white man was born to be the master and the black man was created to be his slave

The attempt of the slavery insurrectionists to bring into contempt the great principle of the declaration of independence and their characterizing the men who uttered it and the men who believe in it as "fancy politicians," shews how absolutely antagonist in their principles were those who rebelled in '76 against unconstitutional acts of parliament, and those who in '61 are rebelling against the constitution of the United States. Even in the august year which we are met to celebrate, the principles and reasonings of our fathers commanded the admiration of Europe, and called forth in the house of lords that magnificent eulogy of Chatham, when he said that for himself he must declare that he had studied and admired the free states of antiquity, the master states of the world : but that for solidity of reasoning, force of sagacity and wisdom of conclusion, no body of men could stand in preference to the congress of Philadelphia.

Whatever may be the future of America the past is safe.

The confederates of the slave republic, unrivalled as may be their skill in robbing us of material wealth and power, cannot rob the founders of our union of their glory—cannot filch from us the treasures we possess in their great principles, cannot les-

sen by the tithe of a hair, the truth of and force of their example.

On the contrary, the formation of the Southern confederacy
adds new proof to their farsighted and prophetic sagacity.
Look at the rebel states, plunged into anarchy and war by Jefferson Davis, with a fettered press, free speech silenced, forced
loans, and an army enlarged by conscription, and then listen to
a single passage from William Pinckney, the great orator of
Maryland, which occurs in a speech made in the Maryland house
of delegates, in 1789 : and remember as you listen to it the proof
I have already given you that the so-called Southern confederacy
is a military despotism, extemporized and precipitated on the
people of the South, who have never been allowed to express
their will in regard to the substitution of the Montgomery constitution, for the ancient constitution and government which the
confederates are striving to destroy.

Said Mr. Pinckney :

"That the dangerous consequences of the system of bondage
have not as yet been felt does not prove that they never will be.
* * To me, sir, nothing for which I have not the evidence of
my senses is more clear than that it will one day destroy that
reverence for liberty which is the vital principle of a republic.

"While a majority of your citizens are accustomed to rule
with the authority of despots within particular limits, while your
youth are reared in the habit of thinking that the great rights
of human nature are not so sacred but they may with innocence
be trampled on, can it be expected that the public mind should
glow with that generous ardor in the cause of freedom which
can alone save a government like ours from *the lurking demon of
usurpation?* Do you not dread contamination of principle?
Have you no alarms for the continuance of that spirit, which
once conducted us to victory and independence when the talons
of power were unclasped for our destruction? Have you no
apprehension that when the votaries of freedom sacrifice also at
the gloomy altars of slavery, they will at length become apos-
tates from the former? For my own part, I have no hope that
the stream of general liberty will flow forever unpolluted through
the foul mire of partial bondage, or that they who have been

habituated to lord it over others, will not in time be base enough to let others lord it over them. If they resist it will be the struggle of *pride and selfishness*, not of *principle.*"

The hour so philosophically predicted seventy-two years ago has come. The usurping hand is lifted against the most benignant government the world has ever seen. The usurpation is unresisted, the country is precipitated into war and popular government overthrown, and a military rule established, the people, it would seem, have cast to the world the historic memories we this day meet to celebrate. Mr. Russell, the correspondent of the London *Times,* now travelling at the South, treated with every attention, charmed with their courtesy, and evidently inclined to regard their rebel movement with a favorable eye, writes from South Carolina on the 30th April, and makes this sad disclosure : " From all quarters have come to my ears the echoes of the same voice ; it may be feigned, but there is no discord in the note, and it sounds in wonderful strength and monotony all over the country. Shades of George III., of North, of Johnson, of all who contended against the great rebellion which tore these colonies from England, can you hear the chorus which rings through the state of Marion, Sumpter and Pinckney and not clash your ghostly hands in triumph? that voice says ' If we could only get one of the royal race of England to rule over us we should be content.' "

Let me say next a word of the means by which a conspiracy so contemptible in its origin, so destitute of moral weight and of popular support has attained to its present dimensions, ousting the federal government of its jurisdiction in more than half of our national territory to the East of the Rocky Mountains, and obtaining possession of arsenals and navy yards and fortresses, seventeen in number, which had cost the American people more than seven millions of dollars.

On the 29th October, 1860, before the presidential election, lieut. general Scott wrote a letter to president Buchanan in which he referred to the secession excitement which the leaders of the conspiracy. were actively fanning at the South, and remarked, that if this glorious union were broken by whatever line political madness might contrive, there would be no hope of reuniting the fragments, except by the laceration and despotism of the sword ; pointing out the danger, he proceeded to point out the prevention.

"From a knowledge of our southern population," he said, "it is my solemn conviction that there is some danger of an early act of rashness preliminary to secession, viz.: the seizure of some or all of the following posts : Forts Jackson and Philip in the Mississippi, below New Orleans, both without garrisons ; Fort Morgan, below Mobile, without a garrison, Forts Pickens and McRae, Pensacola harbor, with an insufficient garrison for one ; Fort Pulaski below Savannah, without a garrison ; Forts Moultrie and Sumpter, Charleston harbor, the former with an insufficient garrison, and the latter without any, and Fort Monroe, Hampton Roads, without a sufficient garrison. In my opinion all these works should immediately be so garrisoned as to make any attempt to take any one of them, by surprise or coup de main, ridiculous.

"With an army, faithful to its allegiance and the navy probably equally so, and with a federal executive for the next twelve months of firmness and moderation, which the country has a right to expect—moderation being an element of power, not less than firmness—there is good reason to hope that the danger of secession may be made to pass away without one conflict of arms, one execution or one arrest for treason."

Gentlemen, lieut. general Scott knew well, we all know, that what he recommended Mr. Buchanan to do an honest executive might have done. Again and again in the history of our country have attempts been made to resist the execution of the laws, and again and again has the federal government triumphantly vindicated its supremacy.

The first armed rebellion was that headed by Shay in Massachusetts in the Winter of 1787. The rebels attempted to seize the arsenal, and were met with cannon that killed three and wounded another of their number, and the state militia, under the command of Gen. Lincoln routed their forces, taking many prisoners, and peace was restored not by any compromise but by the enforcement of the laws.

As a Lincoln suppressed the first rebellion, so will a Lincoln suppress the last.

You will readily call to mind other similar occasions, where the federal government by prompt action maintained its supremacy unimpaired.

First came the whiskey rebellion in Pennsylvania during the administration of Washington, to suppress which the president called out fifteen thousand men from three different states led by their governors and general Morgan, whom Washington at first proposed himself to accompany across the Alleghanies.

Next president Jefferson crushed in the bud the opening conspiracy of Aaron Burr.

President Madison during the war of 1816, when doubts were entertained of the loyalty of the Hartford conventionists, who were falsely reported to be in correspondence with the enemy, stationed major Jessup, of Kentucky, at Hartford with a regiment to suppress any sudden outbreak. Gen. Jackson, about the same time in New Orleans, proclaimed martial law in consequence of attempts by the civil authorities to embarrass the necessary measures of defence.

President Jackson, in 1832, repressed by the arm of general Scott, and amid the hearty applause of the nation, the defiant nullification of South Carolina, and president Tyler, in 1843, with the approval of his secretary, Mr. John C. Calhoun, sent United States troops to Rhode Island to suppress the state revolution organized by a majority of the people of the state, but in violation of the existing state constitution, under the leadership of governor Thomas W. Dorr.

When in 1860 general Scott, in advance of any outbreak, recommended president Buchanan to reinforce the forts instead of recommending active measures of interference, such as his predecessors whom I have named did not hesitate to take, he simply asked of the president to do what any intelligent school boy could see was absolutely proper and essential—and what he could accomplish by a single word.—Mr. Buchanan guided by his secretary of war, the traitor and thief John B. Floyd, refused to order the reinforcement of the fortresses; all the forts named by general Scott, excepting fort Pickens, were seized by the confederates;

and on the fact of their quiet possession, and the aid and comfort thus given to the rebels by the federal cabinet, was based the secession of the traitorous states and the formation of the new confederacy.

The fact thus becomes clear as day, that not simply all the strength the rebel confederacy originally possessed but its very organization and existence, were due not to the people of the South on whom without their sanction it was precipitated, nor to the leaders, skillful as they may have been, who had neither arms nor armies to overpower the government, but they were due to the federal executive and his advisers of the cabinet. This fact is so interesting as a matter of history, it is so important to a right understanding of the whole subject, and bears so clearly upon the question, what is our duty as citizens and what the policy of our government, as regards the tolerance or suppression of this rebellion, that you will allow me to quote one authority upon the point from among the rebels themselves.

The Baltimore *Examiner* in an elaborate eulogy of Floyd, who in the extent and infamy of his treachery certainly excelled his fellow traitors in the cabinet, makes this plain avowal. " All who have attended to the developments of the last three months and knew aught of the movements of the Buchanan administration up to the time of Floyd's resignation, will justify the assertion that the southern confederacy would not and could not be in existence at this hour, but for the action of the late secretary of war.

" The plan invented by general Scott to stop secession was like all campaigns devised by him, very able in its details and nearly certain of general success. The Southern states are full of arsenals and forts commanding their rivers and strategic points : general Scott desired to transfer the army of the United States to these forts as speedily and as quietly as possible. The Southern states could not cut off communication between the government and the fortresses without a great fleet, which they can not build for years ; or take them by land without one hundred thousand men, many hundred millions of dollars, several campaigns, and many a bloody siege. Had Scott been able to have got these forts in the condition he desired them to be, the southern confederacy would not now exist."

Such is the truth fairly stated by the Baltimore *Examiner*, in the interest of the rebels. The union has been severed, not by violence from without, but by treachery within. It has been convulsed from its centre to its circumference, not from any internal weakness in our federal system, but by the infernal villainy of our federal rulers.

Traitors have betrayed the union, traitors have betrayed our forts; and the betrayal no more proves moral weakness in the one case than it does material weakness in the other. There is no fortification so impregnable but that a traitorous governor may yield it without a blow—neither is there any government on God's earth, that secret treachery may not enfeeble or temporarily overthrow.

"If," said Webster, "those appointed to defend the castle shall betray it, woe betide those within. Let us hope," he added, and how vain the hope as regards ourselves! "that we shall never see the time when the government shall be found in opposition to the constitution, and when the guardians of the union shall become its betrayers."

I do not mean to say, gentlemen, that president Buchanan, who, at the close of his administration partially redeemed its character, by calling to his counsels those brave men and true patriots, Mr. Holt and general Dix, was personally privy to the designs of the false secretaries whom they replaced: but it is nevertheless true that he is the man who, under the constitution is directly responsible to the American people for the acts of his administration.

In his position timidity was treason and inaction was crime. He alone could execute the laws, he had the power to execute them, and he did not execute them; and for the simple want of their non-execution the country drifted rapidly towards destruction. This was a case which the founders of our republic had not anticipated. As Mr. Sherman, of Ohio, aptly said, "the constitution provided against every probable vacancy in the office of president, but did not provide for utter imbecility."

I am aware that Mr. Buchanan's friends attribute his conduct

in the whole matter to an amiable credu_ y and a humane desire
to avoid the shedding of a drop of blood. I am sure that none
of us would wish to deprive him of whatever benefit he may de-
rive from the plea of virtuous motives, but allowing them all
the force they are entitled to, we must still exclaim :

"Curse on his virtues, they've undone his country !"

For no other of the confederates in this great villainy will the
candid historian venture with success, the apology of mental imbecility or moral cowardice. They are men who make the boast
that for long years it has been the aim of their existence to overthrow, not by open and honorable opposition, but secretly, trai-
torously and by subornation of treason, the most benignant
government in the world, and one to which they were bound by
solemn oaths and by sacred honor. They are men who, pretend-
ing to be gentlemen, have made conspiracy a trade and perjury
a habit. They have blended professions of patriotism with the
practice of treason, linked the duties of a senator with the position of a spy, and made a seat in the cabinet the office of a thief.
With a refinement of meanness that could belong to no chivalry
but that of slaveholding, and would be practised by no knights
save those of "the golden circle," they have to the last moment
drawn their official salaries from the nation they were betraying ;
they have perfected their schemes of plunder in the very capital
which they were seeking to cripple, and beneath the folds of the
flag that they were swearing to support and plotting to humble.
They are men in brief—for the subject is a revolting one—who,
imitating Judas and rivalling Arnold, have made their daily life
simply and purely a daily lie.

Did time permit me, I would like briefly to refer to the national
evrnts that, following in quick succession, have interrupted what
Mr. Seward happily calls "the majestic march of our national
progress ;" the successive seizure of Southern forts in obedience to telegrams from the senate chamber, the spread of
Southern treason like the wild fire of the prairies, the consterna-
tion of the people, the apathy of the executive, the plot to seize
the capitol, intended to be executed in January and repeatedly
postponed till the attempt involved too serious danger, the sys-
tematic efforts in the departmets of the treasury, of the interior

of war, and I fear also, of the navy, to cripple the United States, to strengthen the rebels, and to close the term of the administration by a *coup d'etat*, that should give to the new confederacy the power and the prestige of the old government, and the preparations made by northern confederates whom the rebels had been taught to believe represented the great northern democracy, for assisting the plot and joining at the right moment in a general revolution.

Lost themselves to a sense of honor, they ceased to believe in its existence at the North. They seem to have been unable to distinguish between a defence of the constitutional rights of slaveholders within the union and under the constitution, and a war in behalf of slavery for the severance of the union, the overthrow of the constitution, the desecration of our flag, and the humiliation of our country. Then came the interruption of their plans by the premature discovery of the theft of the Indian bonds and other villanies, compelling the retirement of the traitorous secretaries Cobb, Thompson and Floyd: the advent of Holt and Dix reviving the hopes of the nation, and the immortal order of the latter, which rung like a trumpet through the land, " If any man shall attempt to pull down the national flag shoot him on the spot."

Then came the official announcement to the country, by the counting of the electoral votes, of the people's choice, next the safe arrival of Mr. Lincoln in Washington, unharmed by the assassins who had sworn to take his life ; then the inuguration, simple and imposing, the oath administered by the chief justice of the United States, and the quiet transfer of such remnants of the federal property as had not been stolen from the people under the retiring administration.

A month of apparent inaction on the part of the new administration, engaged in disentangling the web of treachery, and learning how much of treason lingered in the departments—a month of active preparation by the rebel confederates, and we began to hear the bitter taunts of England at the spiritless people of the great North who were being driven to dissolution and infamy without an effort at resistance, and relinquishing their nationality to a rebellion without striking a blow in its defence.

We had a brief foretaste of the ignominy that awaits a nation which basely surrenders its integrity and its independence, and we heard the prelude of the shout that would greet the downfall of the union, and the epitaph that should record :

* * " But yesterday it might
Have stood against the world ; now lies it there
And none so poor to do it reverence."

Assured of the integrity and patriotism of the President and the wisdom of his cabinet, the North waited as only a brave people, conscious of their strength and of the justice of their cause could afford to wait. The strength of the government was gradually developed, the war and navy departments began to exhibit signs of life—and the great statesman of the West, who sacrificing poltical ambition and personal preferences, had consented to preside over a depleted Treasury, renewed the miracle attributed by Webster to Alexander Hamilton : "He smote the rock of the national resources, and abundant streams of revenue gushed forth. He touched the dead body of the public credit, and it sprang upon its feet."

Desperate as our situation seemed, capitalists demanded no other security than the name of Chase, and when he asked for a loan of eight millions, more than thirty millions were instantly offered.

Gentlemen, I have not time to dwell on the attack on Sumpter, the attack of ten thousand men on one hundred men, and the ill-judged boast of Governor Pickens that they had humbled the star-spangled banner for the first time in seventy years. They themselves by that act and that boast initiated an irresistible conflict that will hardly cease till the stars and stripes again float in their beauty from every fortress in our land.

That bombardment, as was remarked by one of the Judges of the supreme court, "blew all the plots ot the traitors into the air, and inaugurated a change in the sentiment of the country that seemed all but miraculous." It awoke the deep love of country which had slumbered beneath the platforms of party and commercial interest. It ended at once the absurd cry of "no coercion," as applicable to a government in enforcing its laws, and protecting its existence. The rebels by that act closed the door of compromise and reconciliation which had thus far been kept open. They rejected the appeal to a convention of the American people, to which the president in his inaugural had assented—they selected instead the arbitrament of force, the great trial by battle. They struck at the very heart of the nation when they sought to humble the flag of our union that had protected them from infancy, and which from childhood we have loved. They themselves inaugurated war. They imposed upon us the most sacred duty that can devolve upon a people of protecting their nationality, and the world that had wondered at a forbearance which they could not understand, now wondered again at the spontaneous uprising of a mighty nation.

The threatened attack on Washington, the disloyalty of Baltimore, the cutting off of all communication by railroad and telegraph between the national capital and the great North, completed the work begun at Sumpter.

Party lines grew faint and vanished as completely as though they had never existed. Washington has been described as leaning in the darkest hour of the revolution, with one arm resting on Massachusetts, and the other on North Carolina. The faithlessness of the latter to her historic memories, prevents the parallel being now complete, but we may say of Lincoln what can be said of no other president since Washington, that in this dark hour he rests with one great arm upon his political friends, and the other on his political opponents, and that, as he looks abroad over the country whose destinies are in his keeping, he sees neither republicans, nor democrats—neither nativists, nor aliens, he sees but two classes, loyal citizens on the one side, and traitors on the other.

The feeling exhibited throughout the loyal states is not as some Europeans have supposed, an ebulition of enthusiasm, based upon sudden and evanescent passion, but the expression of a profound conviction gradually forced upon them by a long train of facts that culminated at Sumpter, that both duty and honor imperatively demand that they shall crush this gigantic conspiracy against the integrity of the country.

It was this that, within six weeks, called forth, as if by magic, an army of 200,000, converting our cities into camps and making the repression of this rebellion the one great business of the American people.

The scene has been one which, day by day, has thrilled us with emotion, one upon which the Bancroft and the Motley of the next century will linger with admiration.

Massachussetts first in the field, as in the olden days of trial, shedding the first blood at Baltimore, first to occupy and protect the capital, where her great senator was stricken down, against the traitors, whose hatred to him foreshadowed their hatred towards the American constitution, of which he had been the faithful and eloquent expounder.

New York, "herself the noblest eulogium on the union," following close behind with her gallant Seventh, reaching Washington by a march already famous, and insuring by their presence the safety of Washington. The New England states, Pennsylvania and the great west, pouring in their quotas with generous rivalry, and our foreign population rising instantly to the grandeur of the occasion, and hastening to the defence of their adopted country, present features of strength in the American republic of which the most ardent of its eulogists had hardly dreamed.

If any man has regarded our large foreign element as one that threatened danger to the perpetuity of popular institutions, let him glance at the regiments now gathering to battle in their behalf. He will find among them men who have fought for freedom in other lands, and who have pined for their love of it in continental dungeons. He will find scholars from far-famed universities, and graduates of the military schools of Europe who have emerged from positions in which they were gaining an independency to proffer to their country their dear bought experience, and guide and instruct the military ardour that sweeps like a whirlwind over the land. Call the roll of nationalities and you will have responses from England and Ireland, Scotland and Wales, from natives of catholic France and protestant Germany

—you will have replies from Poles who yet dream of an independent Poland, from Hungarians in whose ears still linger the eloquence of Kossuth, from Italians rejoicing in a regenerated Italy, and who are fresh from executing the policy of the lamented Cavour and from fighting by the side of Garibaldi. Every people of Christendom has its representatives in the army of the union that has gone forth to fight for national unity, national independence and the rights of human nature, against the confederated forces of slavery and treason.

In this crisis of our national history it is natural that we should regard with interest the view taken of our course by the great powers of Europe, and especially by that country, with which, as colonies, we were so long connected, and which, despite the two wars that have been waged between us, we are accustomed to remember as our mother-land. Mingled with our Dutch and Huguenot ancestry, a very large proportion of the older families of America trace their descent from England, and many who do not are yet connected with her by no common ties. For myself, I may say that I have always entertained for her people an hereditary feeling of attachment, from the fact that my Huguenot ancestors, when they fled from Rochelle after the revocation by Louis XIV. of the edict of Nantz, found upon her soil a welcome and a home : and that one of them volunteering for King William against James II., shed his blood for English freedom at the battle of the Boyne, that great era in English history, ending, as we hope forever her civil wars, from which dates the establishment on a firm basis, of the unity, the strength and the world-wide dominion of the British empire. Such memories, and doubtless, my countrymen, you have many such, descend from father to son undimmed by national revolutions. They inspire sentiments of affection and kinship, that like family heir-looms gather new value from the lapse of time, and instead of fading as years and centuries roll by, seem the more sacred and imperishable from the thought of the generations by whom they have been cherished and who have each in turn added a link to the chain of association.

The recent visit of the prince of Wales, coming to us as the representative of the British nation, characterized, as it was, by the most graceful courtesy and cordiality on his part, and by the heartiest welcome upon ours, with the single exception of the rude treatment he met at Richmond—now the head-quarters of the rebels—had accomplished what no diplomacy could have effected. It seemed to have blotted out the last lingering remnant of ill-feeling, and left on this side the Atlantic at least, the belief that henceforth there was a firm alliance between England and America, not based on treaty stipulations, but upon that heartfelt cordiality which springs from mutual regard, and from a common devotion to the great principles of right which belong to the institutions of both countries and which their example is recommending to the world ; nor should we overlook the belief cherished by many thoughtful men that if in the distant future England should be set upon by the despotisms of Europe, and should require the aid of her American daughter to save her from annihilation, that aid would be promptly, effectively and cordially given.

It is with profound regret that we have seen that friendly feeling suddenly converted into one of intense and bitter disappointment by the conduct and tone of the English government and the ill-judged comments of the English press.

The election of Mr. Lincoln for the first time entitled to the control of the federal government, a party with whose political principles the English people were supposed to sympathize. By a scheme of treachery unparalleled in baseness, a few of the defeated faction holding office in the cabinet, in congress, in the army and in the navy, conspired together to betray the forts arsenals and other property of the government into the hands of their confederates, with the view of destroying the union, and erecting upon its ruins a Southern confederacy, of which slavery is to be the grand permanent and distinguishing characteristic. They accomplish the seizure of the public property without difficulty, for they themselves were entrusted with its guardianship, and they proceed to develop the great conspiracy and organize the rebel government, while the loyal citizens of the United States are helplessly compelled to await the inauguration of the new president. The 4th of March arrives at last, Mr. Lincoln takes the oath to maintain the constitution and the laws, and when in obedience to that oath he orders the rebels to disperse, and calls upon the country for assistance, the loyal states, as one man, prepare to crush the conspiracy and restore the integrity and the honor of the nation. Neither from England nor from any foreign power have we asked or would we accept assistance in regulating our own household, but from England, of all the states of the world, we thought we had a right to expect a ready sympathy, and that moral support which is given by the countenance of a great nation.

The Southern rebels also counted upon the support of England, on the simple ground that her interest in cotton would incline her to their side, but we although well aware of the demoralizing effect of interest upon national principles, still believed it impossible that the British government could consent from pecuniary motives to look with complacency on the progress of a rebellion whose only strength was gained by treachery, and which was avowedly prosecuted for the maintenance of a system which England herself had taught the world to regard with abhorence. In thus believing, we were confirmed by the tone of the English press when the insurrection first began, one of the ablest representatives of which indignantly declared in substance that Manchester and Birmingham would be the first to reject as an insult, the idea that they were to be moved from their position by pecuniary appeals, and that if any British cabinet should sacrifice the anti-slavery principles of the nation to the question of cotton, England would lose, and deservedly lose, her place at the council table of Europe.

The exclamation of Lord John Russell in reply to a question as to the position of England, "For God's sake let us keep out of it," was followed by what is termed a proclamation of neutrality in which British subjects are forbidden to render assistance to either the United States on the one hand, or the states calling themselves the Confederate States on the other, both of which parties are recognized by the proclamation as "belligerents."

The British government is accustomed to preserve an attitude of neutrality towards contending nations, but it would seem that neutrality does not so far interfere with the sympathies and freedom of its subjects as to compel it to issue proclamations against Irishmen enlisting with Francis Joseph, or Englishmen fighting for Victor Emanuel and Garibaldi.

The proclamation in this case is so warmly eulogized by the British press as precisely the proclamation demanded by the crisis, they profess such profound astonishment that the American people are not satisfied with it, and rate so severely Mr. Cassius M. Clay for expressing with western bluntness his frank surprise, that I will dwell for a moment on what seems to be its meaning and effect.

What has the proclamation effected? How did we stand before it was issued, and how do we stand now?

In the case of the United States, the laws of England and its treaty stipulations with our government already forbade its subjects from engaging in a conspiracy to overthrow our institutions. The proclamation, therefore, in forbidding English subjects to fight in the service of the rebels against the United States, simply declared the law as it was already understood; while in forbidding Englishmen to fight for the United States against the rebels, it intervened to change the existing practice, to revive the almost obsolete act of Geo. III. forbidding English subjects from engaging in foreign service without the royal consent, which had slumbered in regard to Austria and Italy, for the purpose of forbidding Englishmen from assisting to maintain in the United States constitutional order against conspiracy and rebellion, and the cause of freedom against chattel slavery.

The first effect of the proclamation, therefore, was to change the position in which England and Englishmen stood to the United States, to the disadvantage of the latter. Before the proclamation, for an Englishman to serve the United States government in maintaining its integrity was regarded honourable ; after the proclamation such service became a crime. The proclamation makes it an offence now for an Englishman to fight for the government at Washington as great as it was for Englishmen before the proclamation to fight for the rebels of Moutgomery. It thus, in a moral view, lowered the American government to the level of the rebel confederacy, and in the next place. it proceeded, in an international view, to place the rebel confederacy on a par with the American government by recognizing them, not as rebels and insurgents to be dealt with by our government as our constitution and laws should determine, but as a *belligerent* power, to be classed with the United States (of which they were but a rebellious fraction) and equally entitled with the United States to the rights of belligerents under the law of nations.

No ingenuity can blind us to these facts :—Before the proclamation, to support our government was an honorable office for the subjects of Great Britain, and the rebels were insurgents with no rights save under the American constitution.. After the proclamation for an Englishman to serve the United States is a crime and the rebels are elevated into a belligerent power—and this intervention of England, depriving us of a support which her practice permitted, and giving the rebels a status and right they did not possess, we are coolly told is neutrality. Dr. Johnson in his famous letter gave us a sketch of a Chesterfieldean patron seeing a man struggling for life in the water, and when he reached ground encumbering him with help. Lord John has taught us the meaning of British neutrality towards a nation supposed to be in like condition. Let us trust that the English people will not endorse the definition.

What would England have said to such a proclamation of *neutrality* from us in her domestic troubles in Canada, in Ireland or in India? What would the English people have thought of a state paper from Washington, declaring it the sovereign will of the people of the United States to remain perfectly neutral in the contest being waged in Hindostan between the British government on the one side and the Mogul dynasty on the other, and forbidding American citizens to enter the service of either of the said belligerents. What would they have thought of the American president intimating with cold etiquette that it was a matter of profound indifference to this government which of the belligerents should be victorious, the king of Oude and Nana Sahib, or Lord Canning and the immortal Havelock. Or is it that the British have become so enamored of rebellion, aye and of treachery too among their sepoys, that they thus court our great mogul and his fellow traitors of Montgomery ?

This queen's proclamation strikes not simply at the moral

position of our government, but according to the English press it strikes also at our right to execute our own laws against piracy ; and we are told by the *London Times* that if we venture to hang under these laws, a pirate who is licensed to plunder and murder by Jefferson Davis's letters of marque, now endorsed by the sovereigns of England and France, it will be regarded as an outrage by the civilized world ; and this gentle intimation comes to us from a nation who are hardly recovered from the effects of of a rebellion, to end which, without staying to ask the opinion of the world, they blew their rebels from the guns.

It was intimated that the British cabinet were puzzled how to act in regard to the United States on the one hand, and her rebel conspirators on the other, and that after a careful search for precedents, one was found in the royal proclamation touching the war between Greece and Turkey, and that on that was based the proclamation which has so displeased and wounded the American people.

It could not have escaped the cabinet in their search for precedents, for we know with what thoroughness such searches are made, that a very similar state of things existed but a few years since between Great Britain and the United States, when the integrity and honour of the British empire were assailed by her Canadian colonists, and she had occasion to learn what in the opinion of the United States constitutes the duties of neutrality towards a friendly nation. Unsuccessful rebellions are soon forgotten, and perhaps many Englishmen may be surprised on being told that the Canadian rebellion was so deeply seated and so widely spread, as seriously to threaten the crown with the loss of the Canadas. Mr. Leader declared in Parliament that all the English government could do, would be to subjugate and hold the principal cities, leaving the country occupied by rebels. The number of British troops under Sir John Colbourne was only 20,000, while the rebels are said to have had 14,000 at Montreal, 4000 at Napiersville, and thousands more in arms in different parts of the Canadas, fierce with indignation at the murder of a party of patriots by Indians in the employ of the British government.

In November '37 two battles were fought between the British

and the rebels, the one at St. Dennis, and the other at St. Charles which was taken from a force of 3,000 Canadians of whom 200 were killed, and 30 wounded.

In December Mackenzie, the head rebel, who seems to have been the prototype of Davis, organized a provisional government, and assuming the right to dispose of "ten millions of acres of land, fair and fertile," took possession of *Montgomery* House near Toronto, with a band of insurgents, and sent a demand to Sir Francis B. Head to dissolve the provincial parliament, and to leave Toronto within fifteen days.

Then came Lord Gosford's proclamation at Quebec, declaring martial law, and denouncing the conspiracy and rebellion, and on the 8th of January 1838 came the first proclamation from president Van Buren. After reciting the efforts made by him and by the governors of New York and Vermont to prevent any *unlawful interference* on the part of our citizens in the contest unfortunately commenced in the British provinces, and nothwithstanding the presence of the civil officers of the United States who by his direction, had visited the scenes of commotion, arms and amunition have been procured by *the insurgents*, in the United States, the proclamation proceeded :

" Now, therefore, to the end that the authority of the laws may be maintained and the faith of treaties observed, I, Martin Van Buren, do most earnestly exhort all citizens of the United States who have violated their duties to return peaceably to their respective homes, and I hereby warn them that any persons *who shall compromise the neutrality of this government by interfering in an unlawful manner* with the affairs of the neighboring British provinces will render themselves liable to arrest and punishment under the laws of the United States," &c., &c.

At the request of Lord Durham, Mr. Van Bruen had directed our commanding officer on Lake Ontario to co-operate in any measures which might be suggested by Lord Durham for rooting out the band of pirates who had their quarters among " the thousand isles," without the slightest regard to the official proclamation of their chief, Mr. William Johnson, holding a commission from the patriot government, that the patriots would carefully respect neutral waters and the rights of all citizens of the United States.

On the 21st November, 1838, president Van Buren issued a second proclamation, calling upon the misguided and deluded persons to abandon projects dangerous to their own country, fatal to those whom they profess a desire to relieve, impracticable of execution without foreign aid, which they cannot rationally expect to obtain, and giving rise to imputations, however unfounded, against the honor and good faith of their own government.

The proclamation further called upon " every officer, civil and military, and upon every citizen, by the veneration due by all freemen to the laws which they have assisted to enact for their own government, by his regard for the honour and good faith of his country, by his love of honour and respect for that sacred code of laws by which national intercourse is regulated, to use every power to arrest for trial and punishment every offender against the laws providing for the performance of our obligations to the other powers of the world."

On the 4th of December, 1838, the president, in his message to congress, declared, "If an insurrection existed in Canada the amicable disposition of the United States, as well as their duty to themselves, would lead them to maintain a strict neutrality, and to restrain its citizens from all violation of the laws which have been passed for its enforcement. But the government recognises a still higher obligation to repress all attempts on the part of its citizens to disturb the peace of a country where order prevails or has been re-established."

Such was the neutrality on the part of the United States towards Great Britain. It recognized the rebels of Canada not as *belligerents*, but as *insurgents*, and it enforced its neutrality not by forbidding its citizens to assist Great Britain to maintain its authority against the insurgents, but by forbidding them to interfere *in an unlawful manner* with the affairs of the provinces.

It needs no intimate knowledge of international law, no study of Grotius, or Puffendorf, or Vattel, or Wheaton, no definitions of the rights of belligerents and privateers from the *Consolato del Mare*, from Lampredi, Galiani, Moser or Hübner, to enable us to appreciate the wide difference between the neutrality we practiced towards England and her rebels, and that which England has inaugurated against us; and no refinement of reasoning, nor subtle glosses indulged in by the English press, have at all blinded the American people to the unfriendly character of this royal proclamation.

The recognition of the independence of the southern confederacy is a matter in the discretion of England, and of all foreign nations. When this independence is established as a matter of fact we expect it to be recognized, but England does not so recognize it. She recognizes the confederacy as simply struggling for independence as were the insurgents in Canada, and pending the struggle she volunteers under professions of neutrality to ignore our constitutional right to subdue them, and to recognize their rebellion as lawful war. Bound to us by treaty stipulations, she elevates them to an equality of position as regards belligerent rights under the law of nations. She places their usurped government, based on treachery and slavery, on a par with that founded by Washington and his associates on the broad consent of the American people. She introduces Jefferson Davis and his confederates to a limited extent into the family of nations, endorses the licenses given by them to pirates whose brutal cupidity is stimulated by bribes of blood money—twenty dollars for every murdered American! and transforms them into letters of marque which the ships of all nations are bound to recognize, respect and obey.

Had she treated them as *insurgents* they would have had no other rights on the sea than had Bill Johnson, the pirate of the St. Lawrence. Having proclaimed them belligerents she has given them a commission not simply to capture American property in American vessels, but to capture on the high seas American property on board of whatever vessel it may be found, and to carry the neutral vessel and cargo into a belligerent port for further examination. She recognizes the right of the men who have robbed our treasury, betrayed our forts and filched our navy yards and arsenals to establish prize courts to decide upon the lawfulness of captures made by their commissioned cruisers, and brought into court for adjudication, and the title to be given by Davis's courts is to be held valid by the law of nations.

This is what the proclamation of neutrality really means. This is the neutrality which England has inaugurated and which France has adopted ; and those two great powers who recently declared in the congress at Paris that privateering is and shall remain abolished,—by royal and imperial proclamation have countersigned letters of marque for the destruction of American ships, and which threaten with spoliation the commerce of the world. The aim and effect of the British proclamation seems to us so clearly unfriendly and injurious, that it is hardly worth while to note the discourtesy of adopting such a policy, and giving it a definite and irreversible shape in advance of the arrival of Mr. Adams, without allowing us the opportunity to offer a word of explanation or remonstrance. Mr. Adams reached Liverpool the 13th of May.—The next day the proclamation was printed in London.

The United States by their neutrality broke the back of the Canadian rebellion, dashed the hopes cherished by the rebels of effective American sympathy, in good faith assisted the British government in maintaining its authority, and restoring order, and thus materially diminished the cost of treasure and of life at which alone their subjection could have been accomplished.

The British government by their neutrality have made our task far more difficult, apart from the injury we may anticipate from the fleet of privateers whose letters are so respectably countersigned. But we learn from this proclamation one lesson, that will be perhaps worth all that it shall cost us : we learn the treatment we may expect, if we fail to maintain our na tional integrity and the honour of our flag.

If a mere supposition that the rebels of Montgomery are likely to be successful, can in a moment dash from the memory of the English government all recollection of past friendship, and induce her in our moment of trial to condescend to a course so different from that we had pursued towards her : what treatment may we not expect from her, and from every other European cabinet, if we ourselves by our conduct admit that we are powerless at home. How will we be treated abroad, if we yield to the threats of a fraction of our own population ? What will be our standing among nations if, consenting to separation, we lose nearly half of our territory, and two-thirds of our Atlantic seaboard, and descend to the position of a third rate power ? Or what respect will be paid us, if to maintain our territory we compromise with rebellion ? If we yield at the cannon's mouth, what the people have deliberately refused at the polls, if we teach the world by such an example that we may be bullied with success, and that when we resist on principle unreasonable demands, it is only necessary to humble our flag, and to threaten Washington, to induce us ignominously to submit ?

Let us discard all reliance upon other help than that of God, a right cause and a strong arm, and let us recognize the stubborn fact that " the government or nation that fails to protect itself against foes, whether foreign or domestic, deserves to erish ingloriously."*

Before leaving the question of England's neutrality, I think we should distinguish between the hasty action of the British cabinet and the deliberate conviction of the British people.

That the heart of that great nation is sound, and that as soon as they understand the motives and manner of this rebellion as you understand them, they will appreciate our position, approve our resolution and wish us God speed in our great work of restoring the federal union to its integrity and its great original principles of freedom, I cannot, I will not doubt.

Already their cabinet has partially atoned for the first proclamation by an order that will prevent the privateers of Davis from entering British ports, and both the government and the people must soon recognise the fact that we have the ability and the will, to crush this rebellion and maintain our integrity, however long the struggle, however great the cost : and that we no more recognise the right of England nor of Europe to dictate to us in this matter, than England would have recognized our right to interfere between her and Nana Sahib. The material interests based on cotton must yield to the national and moral duties that to-day devolve upon the American people, in determining, perhaps for untold ages, the destiny of the American continent.

The English people will see that our resolve to crush the con-

* Guetano Filangieri.

spiracy for the establishment of a slave empire, is not based on any evanescent burst of enthusiasm, but on the most sober calculations of honor, duty, safety and economy : and that it is the true interest of England, her pecuniary her political and her moral interest that the war should be as brief as possible, that the rebels may no longer be deluded into the belief that any true Englishman who understands the history and the object of their rebellion can regard it with other feelings, than those naturally aroused by a policy of fraud treachery and oppression.

That the restoration of the integrity of our union is to be accomplished without a vast expenditure of treasure, and perhaps of blood, no one anticipates. We all know something of the cost of European wars, but we know also our own resources and the immense stake for which we will be fighting. Our fathers fought for seven years for our national freedom, and the spirit abroad throughout our land indicates that their sons if necessary, will fight seven years more to save it from destruction and disgrace. Whether the debt incurred for its preservation shall be hundreds or thousands of millions it will be a sacred legacy to future generations. A debt of five hundred millions, as remarked by an English jour-nalist, would leave this nation less severely taxed than any nation of Europe.

If any man supposes that this republic can be advantageously sundered into two, let him cast his eye upon the map and endea-vour to find a natural line to separate the two confederacies. The geographical formation of our country indicates that it is one : nature has provided no boundary line between the North and the South : no river like the Mississippi, no mountain chain like the Alleghanies, or the Rocky mountains, running from the West to the Atlantic, and forming an Alpine boundary to divide the sections. On the contrary, the father of waters stretches out his great arms to the East and to the West bearing on his bosom to the gulf, the generous products of the valleys which they fertilize, and carrying back in their place the cotton, rice and sugar of our Southern borders, and imports from foreign climes.

The Mississippi, source and channel of prosperity to North and South alike in every mile of its progress : on the West to Minnesota, Iowa, Missouri, Arkansas, and Louisiana ; on the East to Wisconsin, Illinois, Kentucky, Tennessee, and Mississippi, pro. claims to the citizens of the immense region which it waters through thousands of miles, in extent, from North to South, and East to West, that our country is one and indivisible.

Our duty to the South forbids our acquiescence in this rebellion, for it would reverse the American policy for the last half' century, and reconsign to foreign invasion, to anarchy and ruin, the immense territories which we have rescued from European sway, and united as parts of our great nation.

Look back to the olden time and see what the Southern country would again become. Trace the history of Florida from the days of Charles V., from the adventures of De Leon and De Soto, the persecution of protestants from France, and the retaliation on the murderous Spaniards ; the capture of St. Augustine by Sir Francis Drake, the buccaneering inroads of the English, the transfer of Florida to the British crown ; its partial settlement from Italy and Greece, the privateering exploits in our revolution, the capture of Baton Rouge and Pensacola, until its purchase by our government in 1819.

Remember that the Spaniards navigated the gulf of Mexico for two centuries, without discovering that it was the outlet of the great river of the North, a fact which perhaps induces the Southern confederates to imagine that we also may be persuaded to forget its existence. Look at Louisiana from the days of Law and the Mississippi bubble to its cession to Spain in 1762, and its retrocession to France in 1800, when we hastened to buy it from the first consul, and you will find nothing in Florida, in Louisiana, nor indeed in Texas, to indicate even the first beginning of the prosperity which has been so rapidly developed under the fostering protection of the federal government.

Let the American union be dismembered, and what is to prevent foreign powers from re-entering upon our national domain from which at such great cost and labour they have been ousted ?

An old officer of the French empire writing to the *Courrier des Etats-Unis*, has predicted that in the first place France would retake Louisiana, according to ancient treaties, that Spain would reclaim Florida, that England perhaps would seek to appropriate

Oregon, and that Mexico, under foreign protection, would retake New Mexico, Texas and California; or supposing that we should consent to the establishment of the so-called Southern confederacy, which we know to be a mere military despotism, what possible guarantee can we have for peace in the future, when each state reserves the right to secede at pleasure and enter at will into foreign alliances inaugurating universal chaos and chronic dissolution! Even now, while the struggle is being waged, the leading men of South Carolina, already sick of their independence before it is accomplished, repudiate republican institutions and sigh for a British prince to lend the odour of royalty to the aristocracy which they boast—an aristocracy based not upon historic deeds and noble heroism, but simply upon the colour of their skins, and their despotic dominion over helpless slaves :—an aristocracy whose wealth is invested in human flesh, and whose revenues are collected in the field by the lash, and on the auction block by the hammer !

Let our union be divided with the view of accomplishing present peace, and not only would the United States fall from her position of a first class power to that of a minor republic, with a contracted sea-board and a defenseless border : but the act of separation would inaugurate an exposure to hostilities,—first from our new and unfriendly neighbour, and then from every foreign power with which one or all of the Southern states might choose to form an alliance. Either contingency would necessarily change our national policy, require the maintenance of a standing army, and complicate endlessly our commercial relations. Now, we stand aloof from the quarrels of the rest of the world and can devote our energies to the development of our marvellous resources and the extension of civilization and freedom over the American continent ; then we should be compelled to an attitude of perpetual self-defence to save us from constant entanglement in the web of European politics. Already have we had a foretaste of the sort of treatment which Europe will accord to the severed fragments of the American republic.

To maintain the respect of the world we must maintain first the integrity of our national territory, and next the integrity of our fundamental principles. As for the argument that if the rebellion is crushed harmony can never be restored, Canada furnishes the refutation. The bloody feuds of 1838 have hardly left a trace to mar the tranquil prosperity which marks the progress of that great province. There is reason to believe that the union men of the South await but the coming of the federal forces in sufficient stength, to show themselves again the cordial supporters of the federal government. But even if this were not so, and there was reason to fear a long period of distrust and disaffection, the fact remains that the interests of the American people imperatively demand that the integrity of the union shall be preserved, whether the slavery propagandists of the South like it or like it not.

This is one of those decisive epochs that occur in the history of all great nations. One came to our fathers in 1776. Submission to usurped authority, or national independence, was the issue : and on the day we commemorate they chose the latter ; and the force of their example on the world is yet to be determined. To day the imperious demand comes from slavery, " submit or be destroyed !" Already has a blow been struck by slavery at our republic the force of which reverberates through the world. Two hundred millions of debts due from rebels to loyal citizens are repudiated, the business of the country is arrested, bankruptcy stares us in the face ; worse than all, our flag has been insulted, our prestige impaired, and, from foreign courts, we have received treatment that our American pride can illy brook. Honour, interest, self-respect and the highest duty call upon us to crush, and crush speedily, the insolent traitors whose secret and atrocious perfidy has temporarily crippled us : and while we recall the motives that combine to compel us to resistance, let us not forget the duty which this nation owes to the oppressed race who are the innocent cause of all our troubles, and who have no friends to look to but ourselves, to prevent the spreading of slavery over every foot of American territory, and the waving of the flag of the slave trader over the fearful horrors of the middle passage.

Gentlemen, as in our revolutionary struggle our fathers had to contend with the timid and the avaricious, who feared the evils of war and continually cried peace ! peace ! where there was no peace, so may we expect to be constantly hampered by declaimers in favor of compromise. I do not stop to consider the fitness of our lending an ear to such a cry until the insult to our flag has been atoned for and until our supremacy is acknowledged, for the great mass of the people of the country will be unanimous on this point; they will regard the bare suggestion of treating with the rebels whose hands are stained with the blood of the sons of Massachusetts, of Ellsworth and of Winthrop, of Greble and of Ward, as a personal insult, and will reply to it as did Patrick Henry—"We must fight! I repeat it, sir, we *must* fight!" The sword is now the only pen with which we can write "peace" in enduring characters on the map of America.

The day of compromise is gone : "that sort of thing," as the secretary said, " ended with the fourth of March." We have had devices enough for saving the union, devices suggested by the men who are now striving to destroy it.

There is one good old plan provided by the constitution that was successfully practiced by Washington and Jackson : we are about to try *that* : let us try it thoroughly ; it is simply the due execution of the laws by whatever degree of force the exigency may require. If our army of 300,000 men is insufficient, a million stand ready to follow them to the field.

It would be difficult, my countrymen, to exaggerate the solemn importance of our national position. A struggle for life and death has commenced between freedom and slavery, and on the event of the struggle depends our national existence. Let us falter, let us compromise, let us yield : and the work of our fathers and the inheritance of our children, our own honor and the hopes of the oppressed nationalities of the world will be buried in a common grave! Let us be demoralized by defeat in the field, or what is infinitely worse, by submission to rebellion, and in foreign lands a man will blush and hang his head to declare himself an American citizen. A whipped hound should be the emblem of the Northern man who whimpers for a peace that can only be gained by dishonour.

But let us remember our fathers who, eighty-five years ago, this day, made universal freedom and equal right, the corner stone of this republic ; let us exhibit, as we have begun to do, their stern resolve and high devotion in behalf of constitutional freedom, and we shall secure for our children and our children's children a gigantic and glorious nationality, based upon principles of Christian civilization, such as the world has never seen before.

There is nothing impossible, nothing improbable in our speedy realization of a glorious future.

The seeds of this rebellion have long lurked in our system : for years it has been coming to a head, and simply from want of proper treatment, it has now burst with angry violence : but the pulse of the nation beats cooly and calmly, the partial locallin-flammation but serves to exhibit the lusty health of the body politic, and when this rebellion is extinguished, and its cause re-moved, we may hope that we are safe from an organized rebel-lion for at least a century to come.

With what speed this rebellion shall be crushed, depends sole-ly upon yourselves. Let public feeling lag throughout the land, and the war department will lag in Washington. Let us become careless and indifferent about the matter, and contractors will cheat our soldiers, incompetent officers will expose them to de-feat, official indifference will produce general demoralization.

But let us keep ever in mind the lesson we have so dearly learned —that eternal vigilance is the price of liberty. Let the administra-tion and the army feel that their every act is canvassed by an intelligent people, and when approved, greeted by a hearty ap-preciation : that every branch of industry awaits the ending of the war, and that from every part of the land comes the cry of "forward," and the arm of the union at Washington will obey the heart of the nation, whenever a prayer rises in its behalf, or its flag kisses the breeze of heaven.

Let us with this sleepless vigilance on our part, repose a gene-rous confidence in our president who has won the generous ap-plause of his democratic opponents, nor scan too impatiently the warlike policy of Scott.

Like all true-hearted and brave veterans he wishes to spare as far as possible the blood alike of loyal soldiers and deluded rebels, and to carry with the flag of our union not simply the power to make it respected but the more glorious attributes that cause it to be loved. "Not," to adopt the words of Gov. Andrew, of

Massachussetts, "to inaugurate a war of sections, not to avenge former wrongs, not to perpetuate ancient griefs or memories of conflict," will that flag move onwards until it floats again in its pride and beauty over Richmond and Sumpter, and Montgomery, and New Orleans : but to indicate the majesty of the people, to retain and re-invigorate the institutions of our fathers, to rescue from the despotism of traitors the loyal citizens of the South, and place all loyal or rebel, under the protection of a union that is essential to the welfare of the whole.

The eyes of the whole world are this day fixed upon you. To Europeans themselves, European questions sink to insignificance compared with the American question now to be decided. Rise, my countrymen as did our fathers on the day we celebrate, to the majestic grandeur of this question in its two-fold aspect, as regards America, and as regards the world. Remember that with the failure of the American republic will fall the wisest system of republican govrnment which the wisdom of man has yet invented, and the hopes of popular freedom cherished throughout the globe.

Let us, standing by our fathers' graves, swear anew and teach the oath to our children, that with God's help the American republic, clasping this continent in its embrace shall stand unmoved, though all the powers of slavery, piracy, and European jealousy should combine to overthrow it ; that we shall have in the future, as we have had in the past, one country, one constitution and one destiny ; and that when we shall have passed from earth and the acts of to-day shall be matter of history, and the dark power now seeking our overthrow shall have been itself overthrown, our sons may gather strength from our example in every contest with despotism that time may have in store to try their virtue, and that they may rally under the stars and stripes to battle for freedom and the rights of man, with our olden war cry, "Liberty and union, now and forever, one and inseparable."

.

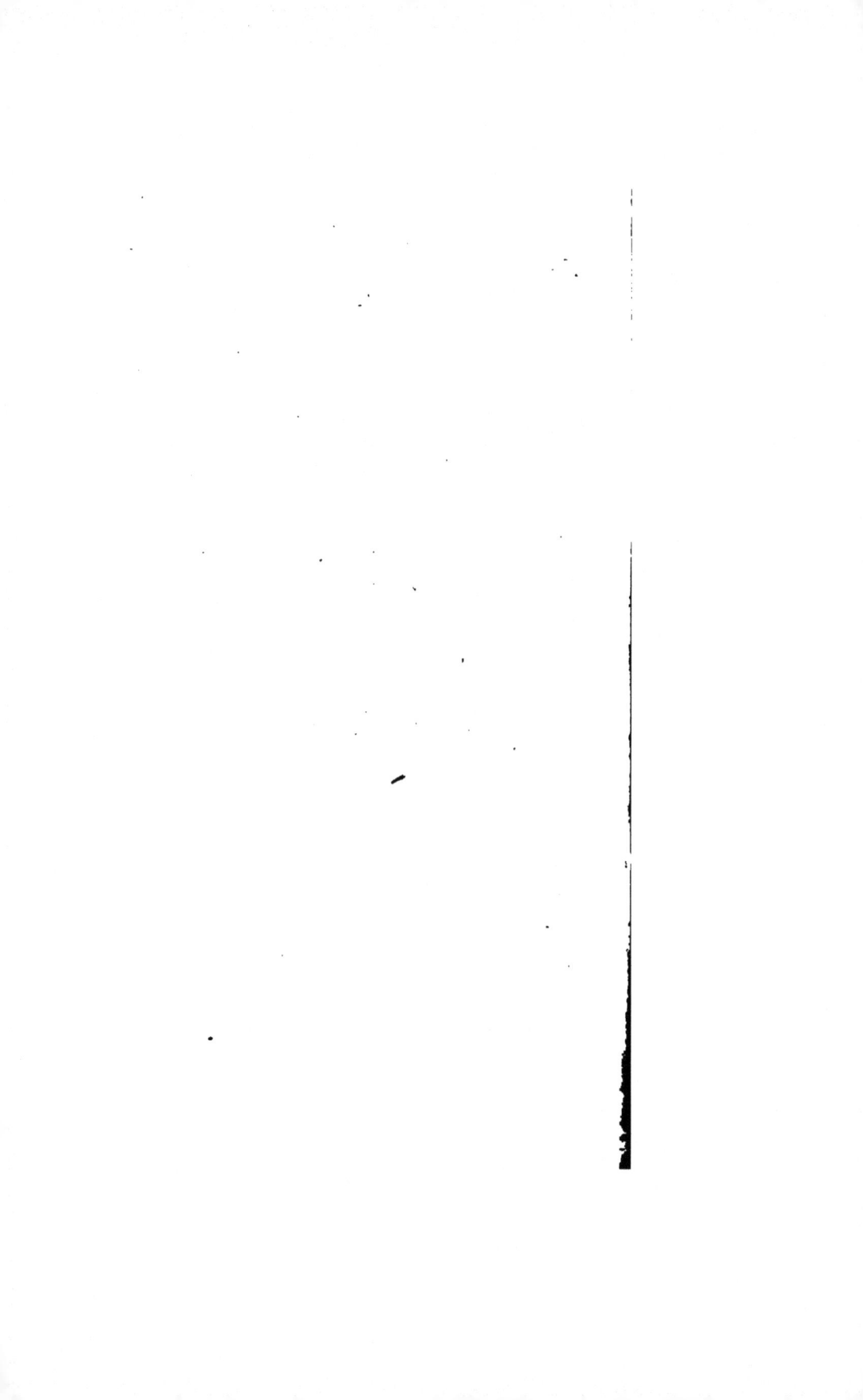

Lightning Source UK Ltd.
Milton Keynes UK
UKOW05n1559120517

301093UK00001B/98/P